WHAT COLOR IS YOUR PARACHUTE?

JOB-HUNTER'S WORKBOOK

A COMPANION TO THE WORLD'S MOST POPULAR AND BESTSELLING CAREER HANDBOOK

SIXTH EDITION

RICHARD N. BOLLES
WITH KATHARINE BROOKS

TEN SPEED PRESS
California | New York

Published in the United States by Ten Speed Press, an imprint of
Random House, a division of Penguin Random House LLC, New York.
www.tenspeed.com

Ten Speed Press and the Ten Speed Press colophon are registered
trademarks of Penguin Random House LLC.

Previous editions of this work were published in 1998, 2005, 2010,
2012, and 2018 by Ten Speed Press, an imprint of Random House,
a division of Penguin Random House LLC.

Library of Congress Cataloging-in-Publication Data is on file with the
publisher.

ISBN: 978-1-9848-5826-9

Printed in The United States of America

Acquiring editor: Lisa Westmoreland | Project editor: Ashley Pierce
Designer: Debbie Berne | Production manager: Dan Myers
Publicist: Lauren Kretzschmar | Marketer: Jessalyn Foggy

The hand with pen on page 16 is by alexblacksea, man with barbell on
page 18 is by makar, light bulb on page 74 is by Nattle.

10 9 8 7 6 5 4

Revised Edition

CONTENTS

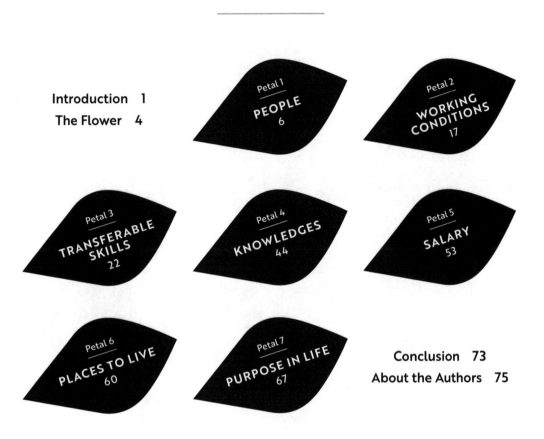

People often say that this or that person has not yet found himself.
But the self is not something one finds,
it is something one creates.

—THOMAS SZASZ

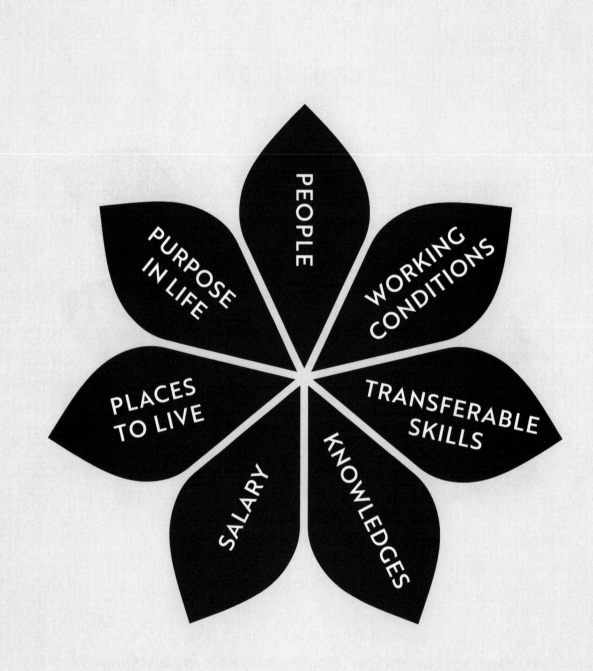

Find what makes your heart sing and create your own music.
—MAC ANDERSON

INTRODUCTION

The Parachute Approach demands that you do an inventory of who you are and what you love to do, before you set out on your search for (meaningful) work.

Being out of work, or thinking about a new job or career, should speak to your heart. It should say something like this:

Use this opportunity. Make this not only a hunt for a job, but a hunt for a life. A deeper life, a victorious life, a life you're prouder of.

The world currently is filled with workers whose weeklong cry is, "When is the weekend going to be here?" And, then, "Thank God it's Friday!" Their work puts bread on the table but . . . they are bored out of their minds. They've never taken the time to think out what they uniquely can do, and what they uniquely have to offer to the world. The world doesn't need any more bored workers. Dream a little. Dream a lot.

How to Do a SELF-Inventory

You begin by stripping yourself (in your mind) of any past job titles. When you ask yourself "Who am I?" you must drop the vocational answer that first springs to mind. Identities such as I'm an accountant, or I am a truck driver, or lawyer, or construction worker, or salesperson, or designer, or writer, or account executive. That kind of an answer locks you into the past. You must think instead "*I am a person who . . .*"

> "*I am a person who* . . . has had these experiences."
> "*I am a person who* . . . is skilled at doing this or that."
> "*I am a person who* . . . knows a lot about this or that."
> "*I am a person who* . . . is unusual in this or that way."

Yes, this is how a useful self-inventory begins. You are a person, not a job.

This self-inventory is a flower with *seven* petals (see pages 4–5). That's because there are seven sides to You, or seven ways of thinking about yourself, or seven ways of describing who you are—*using the language of the workplace.*

If you prefer a different metaphor, you are like a diamond, with seven facets to you, as we hold you up to the light.

1. **You and People.** You can describe *who you are* in terms of the kinds of people you most prefer to *work with or help*—specific qualities, age span, problems, handicaps, etc.

2. **You and a Workplace.** Or you can describe *who you are* in terms of your favorite workplace, or working conditions—indoors/outdoors, small company/large company, windows/no windows, etc.—because they enable you to work at your top form and greatest effectiveness.

3. **You and Skills.** Or you can describe *who you are* in terms of what you can do, and what your *favorite* functional/transferable skills are. For these are key to your being in top form and at your greatest effectiveness.

4. **You and the Knowledges You Already Have.** Or you can describe *who you are* in terms of what you already know—and what your *favorite* knowledges or interests are among all that stuff stored away in your head.

5. **You and Salary/Responsibility.** Or you can describe *who you are* in terms of your preferred salary and level of responsibility—working by yourself, or as a member of a team, or supervising others, or running the show—that you feel most fitted for, by experience, temperament, and appetite.

6. **You and Geography.** Or you can describe *who you are* in terms of your preferred surroundings—here or abroad, warm/cold, north/south, east/west, mountains/coast, urban/ suburban/rural/rustic—where you'd be happiest, do your best work, and would most love to live, all year long, or part of the year, or vacation time, or sabbatical—either now, five years from now, or at retirement.

7. **You and Your Purpose in Life.** Or you can describe *who you are* in terms of your goals or sense of mission and purpose for your life. Alternatively, or in addition, you can get even more particular and describe the goals or mission you want *the organization* to have, where you decide to work.

I Am a Person Who . . .
Is All These Things

You could choose just one, or two, or three, of these sides of yourself—let us say, "what you already know," or "what you can do," or "your preferred salary"—as your guide to defining what kind of work you are looking for.

But what the Flower Diagram does is describe who you are in *all seven* ways, summarized in one graphic. After all, you are not just one of these things; you are *all* of these things. The Flower Diagram is a complete picture of *You*. All of you. In the language of the workplace.

And believe me, you want the complete picture. I'll tell you why. Let's say there is some job out there that matches just one petal, one side to yourself, one way of defining who you are. For example, let's say this job lets you use your favorite knowledges that you already have. But that's it.

That job doesn't let you use your favorite skills, nor does it have you working with the kinds of people you most want to, nor does it give you the surroundings where you can do your best work.

What would you call such a job? At the very least: *boring*. You would barely be able to wait for *Thank God it's Friday!* Some of us have already sung that song. A lot.

But now let us suppose you could instead find another kind of work that matches all seven sides of you. All seven petals. What would you call *that* work? Well, that's *your dream job*.

So, your complete Flower Diagram is a picture of who You most fully are. And, at the same time it is a picture of a job that would most completely match and fulfill all that you are. Where you would shine, because it uses the best of You.

Make it your goal to completely fill in your Flower. *And try to feel it as a joy rather than a duty.* Determine from the beginning that this is going to be fun. Because it sure can be. And should be.

The Flower

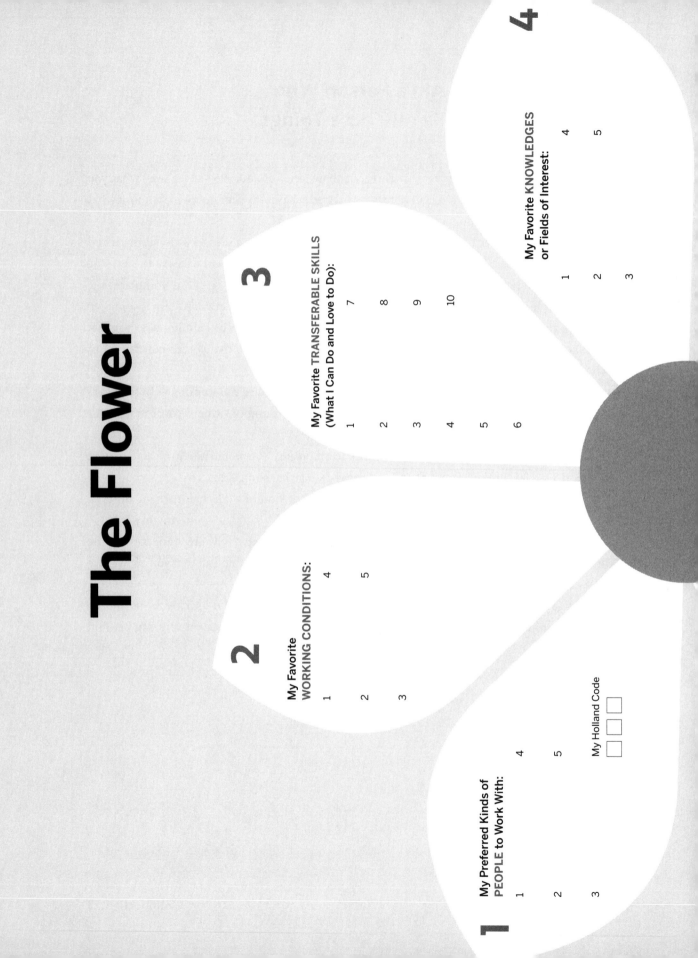

1

My Preferred Kinds of PEOPLE to Work With:

1

2

3

4

5

My Holland Code ☐ ☐ ☐

2

My Favorite WORKING CONDITIONS:

1

2

3

4

5

3

My Favorite TRANSFERABLE SKILLS (What I Can Do and Love to Do):

1

2

3

4

5

6

7

8

9

10

4

My Favorite KNOWLEDGES or Fields of Interest:

1

2

3

4

5

My preferred SALARY RANGE:

Level of Responsibility I'd Like:

Other Rewards Hoped For:

5

My Preferred PLACES TO LIVE:

1

2

3

My Preferred GEORGRAPHICAL FACTORS:

1   4

2   5

3

6

My GOAL, MISSION, or PURPOSE IN LIFE (or my philosophy about life):

7

Knowing yourself is the beginning of all wisdom.

—ARISTOTLE

I Am a Person Who . . .
Has These Favorite Kinds of People

MY PREFERRED KINDS OF PEOPLE TO WORK BESIDE OR SERVE

Goal in Filling Out This Petal: To identify the types of people who can either make the job delightful or ruin your day, your week, your year.

What You Are Looking For: (1) Coworkers and colleagues; a better picture in your mind of what kind of people surrounding you at work will enable you to operate at your highest and most effective level. (2) Clients or customers; a better picture in your mind of what kind of people you would most like to serve or help—defined by age, problems, environment, and so forth.

Form of the Entries on Your Petal: They can be adjectives describing different kinds of people ("kind," "patient") or they can be types of people, as in the Holland Code (see facing page).

Example of a Helpful Petal: (1) People who are creative, smart, fun, and hardworking. (2) People who are engaged in their work and seeking a way to sell or market their product.

Holland Code: IAS. (1) Kind, generous, understanding, fun, smart. (2) The unemployed, people struggling with their faith, worldwide, all ages.

A HEXAGON: THE PARTY GAME EXERCISE

One of the most helpful classifications for determining the type of people you enjoy and the work environment that might best suit you is the Holland Code developed by Dr. John Holland. Every job or career has a characteristic **people environment**. Tell us what **career** or job interests you, and we can tell you, in general terms, what kind of people you would prefer to work with (from among six possibilities). Or start at the other end: tell us what kinds of people you prefer to work with—in terms of those same six factors—and we can tell you what careers will give you *that*. Surveying the whole workplace, Dr. Holland said there are basically six people environments that jobs can give you. Let's tick them off.

1. The **Realistic** People Environment: Filled with people who prefer activities involving the explicit, ordered, or systematic manipulation of objects, tools, machines, and animals.

   *I summarize this as **R** = people who like nature, or plants, or animals, or athletics, or tools and machinery, or being outdoors.*

2. The **Investigative** People Environment: Filled with people who prefer using their brains, specifically the observation and symbolic, systematic, creative investigation of physical, biological, or cultural phenomena.

   *I summarize this as **I** = people who are very curious and like to investigate or analyze things, people, data, or ideas.*

3. The **Artistic** People Environment: Filled with people who prefer activities involving less organized, free-flowing activities and competencies to create art forms or products.

   *I summarize this as **A** = people who are very creative, artistic, imaginative, and innovative, and don't like time clocks.*

4. The **Social** People Environment: Filled with people who prefer activities involving working with others to inform, train, develop, cure, or enlighten.

   *I summarize this as **S** = people who want to help, teach, or serve people.*

5. The **Enterprising** People Environment: Filled with people who prefer activities involving influencing others to attain organizational or self-interest goals.

   *I summarize this as **E** = people who like to start projects or organizations, sell things, or influence, persuade, or lead people.*

6. The **Conventional** People Environment: Filled with people who prefer activities involving the explicit, ordered, systematic manipulation of data, such as keeping records, filing materials, reproducing materials, organizing written and numerical data according to a prescribed plan, operating business and data-processing machines. "Conventional," incidentally, refers to the "values" that people in this environment usually hold—representing the historic mainstream of our culture.

   I summarize this as **C** = *people who like detailed, organized work, and like to complete tasks or projects.*

According to Holland's theory, every one of us *could become skilled* in all six, if we were given enough time. Instead, in the limited time we have from childhood to adulthood, we tend to develop preferences and survival skills in just **three** of these people environments, and this is determined by who we grew up with, who we admired, and what time we gave to practicing expertise in these three people environments, as we wended our way into adulthood. From among the six letters—RIASEC—you name your three preferred people environments, and this gives you what is called your Holland Code; for example, SAI. Your question is, *Which three?*

Generally, most people can just "guess" at their type. (I was friends with John for many years and, back in 1975, I invented a quick and easy way for you to find out your code, based on John's Self-Directed Search [SDS]. It turned out that it agrees with the results you would get from John's SDS 92 percent of the time—this made John laugh.) But if you want a more certain answer, and one of the best ways to learn your code, you can take the free O*NET Interest Profiler online, which will give you your three-letter code (www.mynextmove.org/explore/ip). You can also take Dr. Holland's official SDS ($9.95 at www.self-directed-search.com).

But if you're in a hurry, this is close. And doesn't require access to the internet. I call it "The Party Exercise." Here is how the exercise goes:

The hexagon diagram on the facing page is an aerial view of a room in which a party is taking place. At this party, people who share the same interests have (for some reason) gathered in one of the six corners.

1. To which corner of the room would you instinctively be drawn, as the group of people you would most enjoy being with for the longest time? (Leave aside any question of shyness, or whether you would have to actually talk to them; you could just listen.)

   Write the letter for that corner here

2. After fifteen minutes, everyone in the corner you chose leaves for another party across town, except you. Of the groups that still remain, which corner or group would you be drawn to the most, as the people you would most enjoy being with for the longest time?

    Write the letter for that corner here

3. After fifteen minutes, this group, too, leaves for another party, except you. Of the corners and groups that still remain, which one would you most enjoy being with for the longest time?

    Write the letter for that corner here

The three letters you just chose are your Holland Code.
Put that code here
Now, copy that code onto Petal 1, My Preferred Kinds of People to Work With, found on page 4. So far, so good.

R

R for "Realistic"
People who have athletic or mechanical ability, prefer to work with objects, machines, tools, plants, or animals, or to be outdoors.

I

I for "Investigative"
People who like to observe, learn, investigate, analyze, evaluate, or solve problems.

C for "Conventional"
People who like to work with data, have clerical or numerical ability, carry things out in detail, or follow through on others' instructions.

C

A for "Artistic"
People who have artistic, innovative, or intuitional abilities, and like to work in unstructured situations, using their imagination or creativity.

A

E for "Enterprising"
People who like to work with people—influencing, persuading, performing, leading, or managing for organizational goals or economic gain.

S for "Social"
People who like to work with people—to inform, enlighten, help, train, develop, or cure them, or are skilled with words.

E

S

MY FAVORITE PEOPLE

Why do *the people you prefer* to be around matter at all, in the larger scheme of things? Because the people we work with are either energy drainers or energy creators. They either drag us down and keep us from being our most effective, or they lift us up and help us to be at our best and perform at our greatest effectiveness.

Start, of course, by filling in column 1 in the table on page 12, and then column 2. This will bring you to column 3, where you can fill in the items that you don't like about certain coworkers, clients, and others. In column 4, you will want to prioritize your least favorite kinds of people. How do you do that? Well, you can "eyeball" it and notice which ones jump out at you from column 3, or you can use the Prioritizing Grid. Page 14 shows an example, which illustrates how you use the ten-item grid.

(I originally had more than ten items as a result of this exercise but, by guess and by gosh, I narrowed them down to my top ten and then worked just with them here.)

How to Complete the Prioritizing Grid

Section A. Here I put my list of ten items, in any order I choose. So, as you can see, the people I'd prefer not to have to work with are those who *are bossy, never thanks anyone, messy in dress or office space, claim too much, are uncompassionate, never tell the truth, are always late, are totally undependable, feel superior to others,* or *never have any ideas.* The order in which I list these items here in Section A doesn't matter at all.

Section B. Here are displayed all the possible pairs among those ten. Each pair is in a little box, or rather the *numbers* that represent each pair are in a little box. You ask each box, "Between these two items, which is more important to me?" Or, since this is a grid of dislikes, "Which of these two do I dislike more?" (Think of choosing between two hypothetical jobs.) The framing of the question is crucial.

Let's see how this works. We'll start with the first little box at the top. The box has the numbers 1 and 2 in it. (#1 stands for *bossy*, while #2 stands for *never thanks anyone*). So, the question is, *Which do you dislike more: #1 or #2?* You circle your preference in that box. I circled #1 because I dislike being around bossy people at work more than I dislike being around ungrateful people.

Next, you go on to the second box (down diagonally to the bottom right) that has in it the second pairing—in this case, the numbers 2 and 3. The question, again: Which do you dislike more? I circled #3 in that box because I dislike being around messy people at work more than I dislike being around people who never thank anyone.

And so it goes, until you've circled one number in each little box in Section B.

Section C. Section C has three rows, at the bottom of the grid. The first row is just the ten numbers from Section A.

The second row is how many times each of those numbers just got circled in Section B. As you can see, item #1 got circled seven times, item #2 got circled one time (as did item #10—a tie—so, to break the tie, I look up in section B to find the little box that had both #2 and #10 in it, to see which I preferred at that time, and I see it was #2, so I give #2 an extra ½ point here, over #10). Item #3 got circled three times, but so did item #4 and item #7—*a three-way tie!* How to break that tie? Well, here you'll just have to do some guessing. I guessed these were important to me in this order: #4, #7, and then #3. So I added ½ point to #4 and ¼ point to #7; I left #3 as it was.

In the third and bottom-most row of Section C, I put the ranking according to the number of circles in the second row. Item #6 got the most circles—nine—so it is number 1 in ranking. Item #8 got the next most circles—eight—so it is number 2 in ranking. And so it goes, until that whole bottom line is filled in. Now the only task remaining on this grid is to copy the reorganized list onto Section D.

Section D. The aim here is to relist my ten items (from Section A) in the exact order of my preference or priority, using Section C as my guide. Item #6 got the most circles there, and it ranked number 1, so I copy the words for item #6 in the number 1 position in Section D. Item #8 ranked second, so I copy the words for item #8 into the second spot in Section D. Etc. Etc. What I am left with now, in Section D, is the ten items in the exact order of my preference and priority. *Nice!*

When you've completed the blank grid on page 15 for yourself, go back to the table on page 13. Copy the first five factors from Section D of the grid into the fourth column of the table. Now what you've got there is a list of negatives that you're trying to avoid. But what you want to end up with is a list of *positives* that you're trying to find.

So look at the five negative items you just put in column 4 of the table, and in column 2 write their opposite, or something near the opposite, directly beside each item. By "opposite"

MY FAVORITE PEOPLE

COLUMN 1	COLUMN 2
Places I Have Worked Thus Far in My Life	**Kinds of People I'd Most Like to Work With, in Order of Preference**
	Think back on your favorite people in the workplace. Who supported you? Who always pitched in and helped? Write down the characteristics of your favorite people at work.
	When you finish column 4, return to this column, add in any newly discovered items, and reorder your favorite traits, if needed.
	1.
	2.
	3.
	4.
	5.

MY FAVORITE PEOPLE

COLUMN 3	COLUMN 4
Kinds of People Who Drove Me Nuts	**Kinds of People I'd Prefer Not to Have to Work With, in Order of Preference**
No names, but describe what made them difficult; e.g., bossy, micromanagers, talking too much about their personal problems, always left early before the job was done. List these in any order; it doesn't matter.	Review column 3 or complete the Prioritizing Grid on page 15 and rank your top three to five most difficult people. Consider the opposite trait or characteristic and add that to your list in column 2.

PRIORITIZING GRID
FOR 10 ITEMS OR FEWER

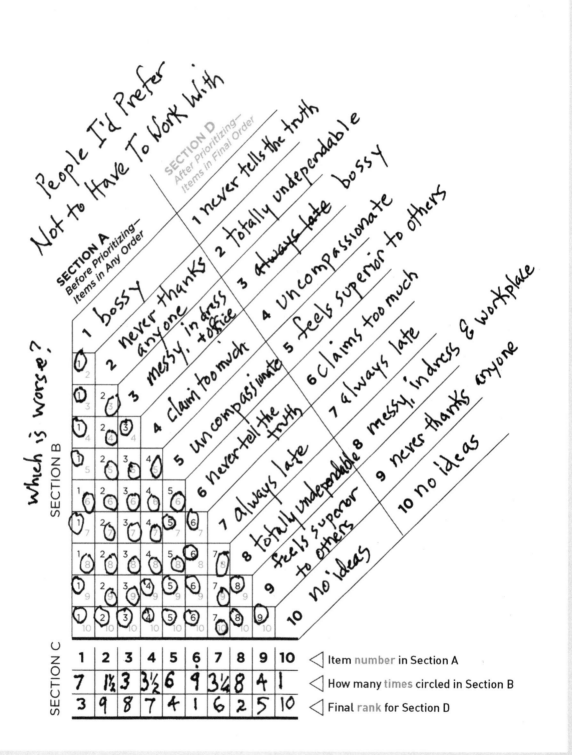

People I'd Prefer
Not to Have To Work With

SECTION A
Before Prioritizing—Items in Any Order

SECTION D
After Prioritizing—Items in Final Order

1 bossy
2 never thanks anyone
3 messy: in dress + office
4 claim too much
5 uncompassionate
6 never tell the truth
7 always late
8 totally undependable feels superior to others
9 no ideas

1 never tells the truth
2 totally undependable
3 always late
4 uncompassionate
5 feels superior to others
6 claims too much
7 always late
8 messy, in dress & workplace
9 never thanks anyone
10 no ideas

Which is worse?

SECTION B

SECTION C

	1	2	3	4	5	6	7	8	9	10
	7	1½	3	3½	6	9	3½	8	4	1
	3	9	8	7	4	1	6	2	5	10

◁ Item **number** in Section A

◁ How many **times** circled in Section B

◁ Final **rank** for Section D

PRIORITIZING GRID
FOR 10 ITEMS OR FEWER

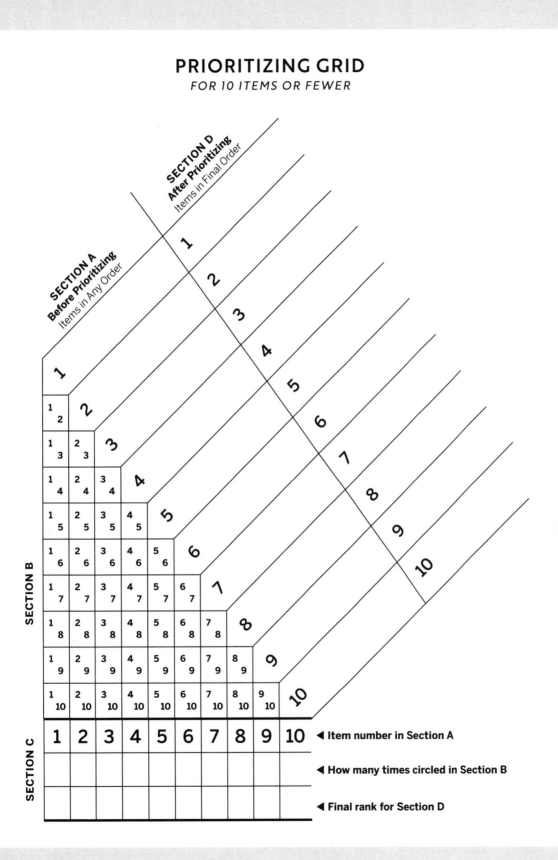

I don't necessarily mean the *exact* opposite. If one of your complaints in column 4 was "I was micromanaged, supervised every hour of my day," the opposite, in column 2, wouldn't necessarily be "No supervision." It might be "Limited supervision" or something like that. Your call. Note that you are adding these items to the list you already compiled in column 1. If there are duplicates, just leave them out. Highlight or place a star next to the positive items that are most important to you in column 1. Too many? Not sure? Then use the Prioritizing Grid again.

Now copy the top five from column 2 onto Petal 1, My Preferred Kinds of People to Work With, on page 4.

Congratulations! You did it—you're done with Petal 1. Take a break or move on to Petal 2.

WORKING CONDITIONS

I Am a Person Who . . .
Has These Favorite Working Conditions

MY PREFERRED WORKING CONDITIONS

Goal in Filling Out This Petal: To state the physical working conditions and surroundings that would make you happiest, and therefore enable you to do your most effective work.

What You Are Looking For: Setting yourself up for a great work environment and avoiding past bad experiences.

Form of the Entries on Your Petal: Descriptors of physical surroundings and general work environment.

Example of a Helpful Petal: A workspace with lots of windows, nice view of greenery, relatively quiet, decent lunch period, flexibility about clocking in and clocking out, lots of shops nearby.

Your physical setting where you work can cheer you up or drag you down. It's important to know this before you weigh whether to take a particular job offer. The most useful way to do this has proved to be starting with working conditions that have made you unhappy in the past and then flip them over into positives, just as we did in the previous exercise.

Plants that grow beautifully at sea level often perish if they're taken ten thousand feet up the mountain. Likewise, we do our best work under certain conditions but not under others.

Thus, the question "What are your favorite working conditions?" actually is "Under what circumstances do you do your most effective work?"

Before you get started, again, this petal is about physical space and location—not people. To add more about people, go back to Petal 1.

PETAL 2, WORKSHEET #1

A TABLE: PHYSICAL ENVIRONMENTS WHERE I WOULD THRIVE

The best way to approach the chart on pages 20–21 is to focus on both the good and bad aspects of previous jobs. Fill in each of the columns as you think about your past work experiences. In column 1, list all the places where you have worked. When you think of something positive ("nice view" or "casual environment"), write that in column 2. When you think of things you would prefer to not experience again ("outdoors in the hot sun" or "cubicle"), write them in column 3. Rank the worst experiences from column 3 (again, by "eyeballing" it or by using the Prioritizing Grid) and write the rank-ordered list in column 4. Then consider the opposite ("indoor air-conditioned environment" or "personal office with walls") and write those items in column 2 if they are not already there. Copy the top five key items from column 2 onto Petal 2, the Favorite Working Conditions petal of your Flower Diagram, pages 4–5. (For some people it's easier to remember all the things you *disliked* about *any* previous job. If that's the case for you, just start with column 3 and go from there.)

PETAL 2, WORKSHEET #2
CREATE A VISION OF YOUR IDEAL WORK ENVIRONMENT

Worksheet #1 helped you organize your thoughts in a logical manner, but your worksheet might be limited by what you already know. Creating a Vision Board of possibilities and ideas could help open your mind to new opportunities. Please keep in mind that this Vision Board is not magic. Its purpose is to help you think visually about your future workplace and expand your thinking with new images. You will still have to set goals and take action to make any "vision" real. You can create your Vision Board in two ways: on paper or online.

Paper version: Get a large sheet of paper or a poster board, then go through magazines, and cut out pictures that fit your ideal environment. Don't censor yourself by saying *there's no point in including that picture. That will never happen.* Glue the picture onto your paper anyway. (If you can't find enough magazines, go online and print out pictures.)

Online version: Instead of using paper, just open a blank Word document and copy and paste pictures from various websites. (One caution: sometimes pictures can have viruses attached to them, so be sure to keep your virus protector active while you're doing this exercise, and consider only using safe picture sites, like Pinterest, Pixabay.com, or Unsplash.com.)

When you're done adding the images you've chosen, analyze your results. Did you collect a lot of certain kinds of images? Are they formal environments or more casual? Are they located in a city or near the seashore? Are there certain elements present, such as a medical/hospital setting, or a college setting, or a modern technology firm?

Sometimes it helps to have your friends or relatives look at your board. They might see trends or spot new ideas that you've missed. When you've completed Worksheet #2, write down the key elements you identified from your board. If there are new insights, consider adding them to column 2 of Worksheet #1 and including them on Petal 2 if they are significant and important factors.

And you're done with Petal 2 for the moment. Keep in mind you can always add extra items as you think about them. It's not unusual to complete a petal one day, only to think of more things to add the next day. This is a living document, so don't hesitate to add more ideas as they occur to you.

Time for a break? Or ready to move on?

PREFERENCES FOR WORKING CONDITIONS

COLUMN 1	COLUMN 2
Places I Have Worked	**The Keys to My Effectiveness at Work— What I Like or Need**
	I believe my effectiveness would be at an absolute maximum if I could work under these conditions.
	(List ideal aspects of previous jobs.)

PREFERENCES FOR WORKING CONDITIONS

COLUMN 3	COLUMN 4
Distasteful Working Conditions	**Distasteful Working Conditions, Ranked**
I have learned from the past that my effectiveness at work is decreased when I have to work under these conditions. (List less desirable or bad conditions you experienced.)	Among the factors or qualities listed in column 3, these are the ones I dislike absolutely the most (rank in order of decreasing dislike). Consider the opposite of these conditions and place those in column 2.
1.	1.
2.	2.
3.	3.
4.	4.
5.	5.

I Am a Person Who . . .
Can Do These Particular Things
in These Particular Ways

MY FAVORITE TRANSFERABLE SKILLS AND TRAITS

Goal in Filling Out This Petal: To discover your favorite functional skills and personal traits, which can be transferred to any field of interest. They are things you probably were born knowing how to do, or at least you began with a natural gift and have honed and sharpened it since.

What You Are Looking For: Not just what you can do but, more particularly, which of those skills and traits you most love to use.

Form of the Entries on Your Petal: Verbs, usually in pure form (for example, analyze, write, draw, coach), though they may sometimes be expressed as actions (for example, analyzing, writing, drawing, coaching).

Example of a Helpful Petal: (These stories show that I can) innovate, analyze, classify, coach, negotiate; or (These stories show that I am good at) innovating, analyzing, classifying, coaching, negotiating.

A Crash Course in Skills, Talents, Abilities, and Traits

"Skills" is one of the most misunderstood words in all the world of work. It begins with high school job hunters. "I haven't really got any skills," they say. *Wrong!*

It continues with college students: "I've spent four years in college. I haven't had time to pick up any skills." *Wrong!*

And it lasts through the middle years, especially when a person is thinking of changing his or her career: "I'll have to go back to college and get retrained, because otherwise I won't have any skills in my new field." Or "Well, if I claim any skills, I'll have to start at a very entry kind of level." *Wrong!*

All of this confusion about the word "skills" stems from a total misunderstanding of what the word means. A misunderstanding that is shared, we might add, by altogether too many employers, and human resources departments, and other so-called vocational experts. So let's clarify what we mean here.

Skills are simply something you are good at. They can also be called talents or abilities. They can also be divided into categories, like "soft" or "hard" or "transferable." Basically, hard skills refer back to the "what," and soft skills refer more to the style in which you do something—the "how." Sometimes soft skills illustrate personality traits. And just to confuse the issue more, sometimes soft skills are also called "self-management skills." And what about "transferable skills"? That basically means that the hard and soft skills—and traits—

that you perform in one setting can be useful in another setting. Sometimes it isn't just the specific skill that is transferable, but rather the thinking required to do the skill.

Finally, there's another term that is becoming more common in the job-search world: "competencies." In many ways, the word "competencies" is just a fancier name for skills, but it is often used to categorize a larger set of skills. For instance, a competency in communications might include writing skills, speaking skills, leadership skills, and so on.

Okay, let's get out of the weeds. In this section, with this petal, we are going to focus on the skills and traits you possess, with an emphasis on which ones are most transferable to other jobs and roles.

It's important to do a thorough assessment of your skills and traits, because too many people assume they don't have the needed skills for a new job and end up returning to school and spending money on a formal degree they might not have needed. I've said it before, and I'll say it again: *maybe* you need some further schooling, but very often it is possible to make a dramatic career change without any retraining. It all depends. And you won't really *know* whether or not you need further schooling until you have finished all the exercises in this self-inventory. Knowing and analyzing your skills seems basic, but it's amazing how many job seekers don't take the time to do this.

All skills have the potential to be transferable. So let's start with some assumptions.

1. **Your skills are the most basic unit—the atoms—of whatever job or career you may choose.**

2. **You should always claim the highest skills you legitimately can, as demonstrated by your past performance.**
When you list your skills (which you will do shortly), consider which skills are the most difficult or complex. Those skills are likely to be more valued by a future employer.

3. **The higher your transferable skills, the more freedom you will have on the job.**
The more complex and valuable your skills are, the more opportunities you will have to carve out a job that truly fits you. For instance, most workplaces and positions require computer or other technical skills. If you know how to use a word processing program, that's a great skill, but it's a skill that many others possess as well. However, if you also know how to use a graphic design program, that is an additional skill that may add to your value to an employer (particularly if you can demonstrate why this skill could help). And if you can also code or write apps, well, then your technical skills are likely to land you a job.

4. **The higher your transferable skills, the less competition you will face for whatever job you are seeking.**
The essence of this approach to job hunting or career changing is that once you have identified your favorite transferable skills and your favorite special knowledges, you may then approach any organization that interests you, whether they have a known vacancy or not. Naturally,

whatever places you visit—and particularly those that have not advertised any vacancy—you will find far fewer job hunters with whom you have to compete.

In fact, if the employers you visit happen to like you well enough, they may be willing to create for you a job that does not presently exist. *In which case, you will be competing with no one, since you will be the sole applicant.* While this doesn't happen all the time, it is astounding to me how many times it *does* happen. The *reason* it does is that the employers often have been *thinking* about creating a new job within their organization, for quite some time—but with this and that, they just have never gotten around to *doing* it. Until you walk in.

Then they decide they don't want to let you get away, since *good employees are as hard to find as good employers.* And they suddenly remember that job they have been thinking about creating for many weeks or months now. So they dust off their *intention,* create the job on the spot, and offer it to you! And if that new job is not only what *they* need but exactly what *you* were looking for, then you have a dream job. Match-match. Win-win.

PETAL 3, WORKSHEET #1
A SKILLS CHART: ANALYZING SEVEN STORIES WHEN YOU WERE ENJOYING YOURSELF

Now that you know what transferable skills *are,* the challenge that awaits you is figuring out your own. If you are one of the lucky few people who already know what their transferable skills are, write them down and put them in your order of preference on your Flower Diagram (pages 4–5).

If, however, you don't know what your skills are (and 95 percent of all workers *don't*), you will need some help. Fortunately, there is an exercise to accomplish that goal.

It involves the following steps.

1. Write One Story (the First of Seven) About Some Episode in Your Life

Yes, I know, I know. You are avoiding this exercise because you don't like to write. *Writers are a very rare breed.* That's what thousands of job hunters have told me, over the years. And yet, how often during the day do you text or email? You are a writer every day and just don't realize it. Let's face it, we human beings are a writing species, and we only need a topic we have a real passion for, or interest in—such as our own life—for the writing genie to spring forth from within each of us, pen or keyboard at hand.

So, identify the *Seven Stories from your life* that you're about to write as your personal *offline blog*, if you prefer. But start writing. Please.

Okay, the next step is actually writing. Here is one person's first story:

Several years ago, our family adopted a mixed-breed puppy from a shelter. Based on her appearance, she seemed to be part Poodle, part Labrador, and maybe part Border Collie. We named her Ruffles. Not only was Ruffles adorable, she had the sweetest, gentlest nature and loved everyone. She was a hit at the local dog park and everywhere I took her. The only challenge was her high energy level: she jumped around and pulled on her leash; she got bored easily and chewed up the furniture, and anything else, if I didn't keep her busy. A friend suggested I get her obedience training, so I enrolled her in puppy kindergarten at a local pet store. We failed miserably. She preferred socializing with the other dogs and people and had no interest in listening to me.

Something about this experience triggered my own stubborn nature, so I decided to train her myself. In fact, I had a secret goal: I would train her to be a therapy dog and take her to a local children's hospital. I started by getting some books from the library on dog training. I watched TV programs on the topic and started trying the various techniques to see which worked best. She was doing great at home, but I still had challenges with her in public. I looked up therapy dog training and discovered that the American Kennel Club has a Canine Good Citizen program for training dogs. The training I had done at home helped Ruffles quickly succeed in the group environment, and she was able to complete the ten-step test (which included sitting politely for petting and ignoring distractions in her environment) and achieve her Canine Good Citizen certificate.

After that, I checked with the local children's hospital and learned that Ruffles and I needed to go through another program to certify her as a therapy dog, so we enrolled in online training through a nonprofit organization. Once she was through the training process and attained her "novice" status, we started visiting the children's hospital.

I didn't realize what a commitment I had made when I set my first goal with Ruffles, but the experience was incredible. I met so many wonderful children and families who were going through a terrible time in their lives, and watching their faces light up when they saw Ruffles was the highlight of my week. As I look back, I think I benefited more than anyone from the experience.

As this example illustrates, each story should have the following points:

- **Your goal/what you wanted to accomplish.** "I wanted my dog to stop chewing up the furniture, and I also wanted to find an outlet for her energy and friendly personality."

- **Some kind of hurdle, obstacle, or constraint you faced.** "She and I failed miserably in puppy kindergarten. She was stubborn and too interested in other dogs and people. I couldn't control her, and I was sure I wouldn't be able to train her."

- **A description of what you did, step by step, to ultimately achieve your goal.** "I read everything I could about training dogs. I watched TV shows, too, and I tried all the techniques. I kept taking her to the park and working on her socialization skills. I searched out local training programs for preparing her to be a therapy dog. I enrolled in several programs both in person and online. I then started taking her to the hospital to try out and improve her skills."

- **A description of the outcome or result.** "Ruffles received the appropriate certificate and was able to volunteer at the local children's hospital."

- **Any measurable/quantifiable statement of that outcome.** "I'd have to say that the outcome is more emotional than financial. I learned a lot about myself, particularly my tenacity and my patience. I also learned a lot about compassion and kindness, and the value of small experiences that can make someone's day. I think working with Ruffles made me a better person."

Now write *your* story, using the space on page 28 and the sample as a guide.

Don't pick a story where you achieved something *big,* like "how I got my college degree over a period of ten years." At least to begin with, write a story about some brief episode or task you accomplished, in which you also had fun!

Do not try to be *too* brief. This isn't Twitter.

MY FIRST LIFE STORY

Your Goal (what you want to accomplish):

Some Kind of Obstacle (or Limit, Hurdle, or Restraint) You Had to Overcome Before It Could Be Accomplished:

What You Did Step by Step:

Description of the Result (what you accomplished):

Any Measure or Quantities to Prove Your Achievement:

2. Analyze Your (First) Story, Using the Skills Grid, to See What Transferable Skills You Used

Above the number 1 in the grid on page 30, write a brief title for your first story. Then work your way down column 1, asking yourself for each skill in the right-hand column: "Did I use this skill in this story?" If the answer is "Yes," color in the little square for that skill, in that column, with a red pen or whatever.

Work your way through the entire Parachute Skills Grid that way, with your first story.

As an example, if we were to analyze the "Ruffles" story to identify some key skills used by Ruffles's owner, we might select training, follow-through, assessing and evaluating, communicating well, problem solving, and plan.

3. Write Six Other Stories, and Analyze Them for Transferable Skills

Voilà! You are done with Story #1. However, "one swallow doth not a summer make," so the fact that you used certain skills in this first story doesn't tell you much. You have to keep writing stories—seven is the ideal, five is the minimum to be of any use—because what you are looking for is patterns—transferable skills that keep reappearing in story after story. They keep reappearing because they are your favorites (assuming you chose stories where you were *really* enjoying yourself).

If you are finding it difficult to come up with seven stories, here are some ideas that might inspire you. Write a story about:

- A situation that made you feel part of something larger than yourself
- An experience that stood out because you were proud of what you accomplished
- Helping someone, or making someone else's life better
- Something you did despite others saying you couldn't do it
- Something that was exciting or inspiring to you
- An experience that taught you something, even if it wasn't fun at the time
- An experience that required you to take a risk

Don't forget to look for skills that you use outside of work. For instance, if you enjoy playing video games, it is possible that you have developed skills such as strategic planning, navigating changing environments, active listening, communicating, or collaborating. Not only are those skills useful in various jobs and fields, but if you want a career in video game development, video game skills can get you a scholarship to college—more than thirty colleges, including NYU, offer scholarships to study gaming.

THE PARACHUTE SKILLS GRID

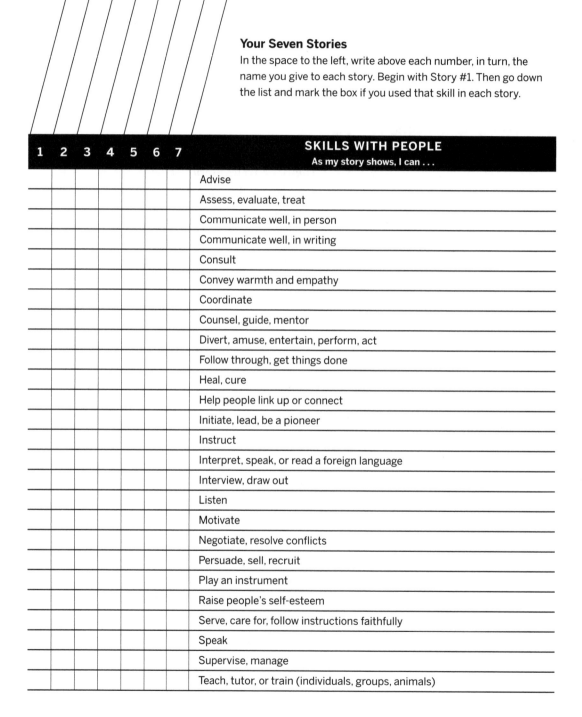

Your Seven Stories

In the space to the left, write above each number, in turn, the name you give to each story. Begin with Story #1. Then go down the list and mark the box if you used that skill in each story.

1	2	3	4	5	6	7	SKILLS WITH PEOPLE As my story shows, I can . . .
							Advise
							Assess, evaluate, treat
							Communicate well, in person
							Communicate well, in writing
							Consult
							Convey warmth and empathy
							Coordinate
							Counsel, guide, mentor
							Divert, amuse, entertain, perform, act
							Follow through, get things done
							Heal, cure
							Help people link up or connect
							Initiate, lead, be a pioneer
							Instruct
							Interpret, speak, or read a foreign language
							Interview, draw out
							Listen
							Motivate
							Negotiate, resolve conflicts
							Persuade, sell, recruit
							Play an instrument
							Raise people's self-esteem
							Serve, care for, follow instructions faithfully
							Speak
							Supervise, manage
							Teach, tutor, or train (individuals, groups, animals)

1	2	3	4	5	6	7	SKILLS WITH DATA/IDEAS As my story shows, I can . . .
							Analyze, break down into parts
							Compile, keep records, file, retrieve
							Copy
							Create, innovate, invent
							Design, use artistic abilities, be original
							Develop, improve
							Examine, inspect, compare, see similarities and differences
							Imagine
							Organize, classify
							Perceive patterns
							Plan
							Program
							Remember people, or data, to unusual degree
							Research
							Use acute senses (hearing, smell, taste, sight)
							Use my brain
							Use my intuition
							Visualize, including in three dimensions
							Solve problems
							Study, observe
							Synthesize, combine parts into a whole
							Systematize, prioritize
							Work with numbers, compute

1	2	3	4	5	6	7	SKILLS WITH THINGS As my story shows, I can . . .
							Control, expedite things
							Construct
							Cut, carve, chisel
							Finish, restore, preserve
							Handle, tend, feed
							Make, produce, manufacture
							Manipulate
							Operate, drive
							Repair
							Set up, assemble
							Shape, model, sculpt
							Use my body, hands, fingers, with unusual dexterity or strength

MY SECOND LIFE STORY

Your Goal (what you want to accomplish):

Some Kind of Obstacle (or Limit, Hurdle, or Restraint) You Had to Overcome Before It Could Be Accomplished:

What You Did Step by Step:

Description of the Result (what you accomplished):

Any Measure or Quantities to Prove Your Achievement:

MY THIRD LIFE STORY

Your Goal (what you want to accomplish):

Some Kind of Obstacle (or Limit, Hurdle, or Restraint) You Had to Overcome Before It Could Be Accomplished:

What You Did Step by Step:

Description of the Result (what you accomplished):

Any Measure or Quantities to Prove Your Achievement:

MY FOURTH LIFE STORY

Your Goal (what you want to accomplish):

Some Kind of Obstacle (or Limit, Hurdle, or Restraint) You Had to Overcome Before It Could Be Accomplished:

What You Did Step by Step:

Description of the Result (what you accomplished):

Any Measure or Quantities to Prove Your Achievement:

MY FIFTH LIFE STORY

Your Goal (what you want to accomplish):

Some Kind of Obstacle (or Limit, Hurdle, or Restraint) You Had to Overcome Before It Could Be Accomplished:

What You Did Step by Step:

Description of the Result (what you accomplished):

Any Measure or Quantities to Prove Your Achievement:

MY SIXTH LIFE STORY

Your Goal (what you want to accomplish):

Some Kind of Obstacle (or Limit, Hurdle, or Restraint) You Had to Overcome Before It Could Be Accomplished:

What You Did Step by Step:

Description of the Result (what you accomplished):

Any Measure or Quantities to Prove Your Achievement:

MY SEVENTH LIFE STORY

Your Goal (what you want to accomplish):

Some Kind of Obstacle (or Limit, Hurdle, or Restraint) You Had to Overcome Before It Could Be Accomplished:

What You Did Step by Step:

Description of the Result (what you accomplished):

Any Measure or Quantities to Prove Your Achievement:

Are you still stuck? If you absolutely can't think of any experiences you've had where you enjoyed yourself, and accomplished something, then try this: describe the seven most enjoyable jobs that you've had; or seven roles you've had so far in your life, such as spouse, parent, tutor, homemaker, handyman, gardener, community volunteer, citizen, student, etc. Tell us something you did or accomplished, in each role. In his excellent book *The Seven Habits of Highly Effective People*, Stephen Covey encourages readers to identify seven roles they play or want to play in their lives. Check out this book if you'd like to learn more about thinking of yourself in terms of roles that you play.

So, write Story #2, from any period in your life, and analyze it using the skills grid. And keep this process up, until you have written, and analyzed, all your stories. A weekend should do it! In a weekend, you can inventory your *past* sufficiently so that you have a good picture of the *kind* of work you would love to be doing *in the future*. (You can, of course, stretch the inventory over a number of weeks, maybe doing an hour or two one night a week, if you prefer. It's up to you as to how fast you do it.)

4. Discover Patterns and Priorities

Okay, when you've finished this whole inventory, for all seven of your accomplishments/achievements/jobs/roles or whatever, you want to look down your completed Skills Grid to discover any **patterns** or **priorities**.

> **Patterns**, because it isn't a matter of whether you used a skill only once, but rather whether you used it again and again. "Once" proves nothing; "again and again" is very convincing.

> **Priorities** (that is, which skills are most important to you), because as we saw earlier, the job you eventually choose may not enable you to use all of your skills. You need to know *what you are willing to trade off, and what you are not.* This requires that you know which skills, or family of skills, are most important to you.

So, after finishing your seven stories (or if you're in a hurry, at least five), look through that Skills Grid and *guess* which *might* be your top ten favorite skills. These should be your best *guesses,* and they should be about *your favorite* skills; not the ones you think the job market will like the best, but the ones *you* enjoy using the most.

At this point, now that you've guessed your top ten, you want to organize those ten *in exact order of priority.* Run your *guesses* through the Prioritizing Grid on page 39, and when you're done with that grid's Section D, copy the top ten onto the building blocks diagram on page 40, as well as onto your Favorite Transferable Skills petal, on page 4.

PRIORITIZING GRID

FOR 10 ITEMS OR FEWER

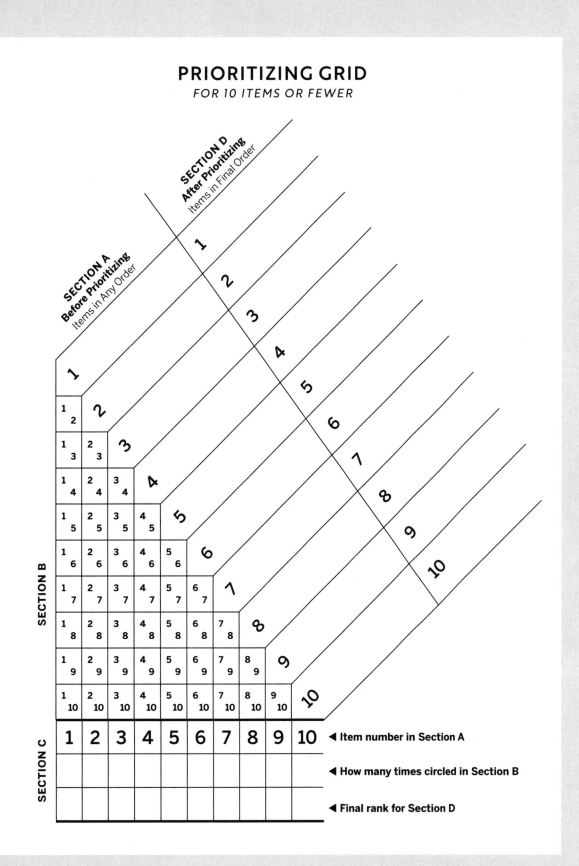

SECTION D
After Prioritizing
Items in Final Order

SECTION A
Before Prioritizing
Items in Any Order

SECTION B

SECTION C

◄ **Item number in Section A**

◄ **How many times circled in Section B**

◄ **Final rank for Section D**

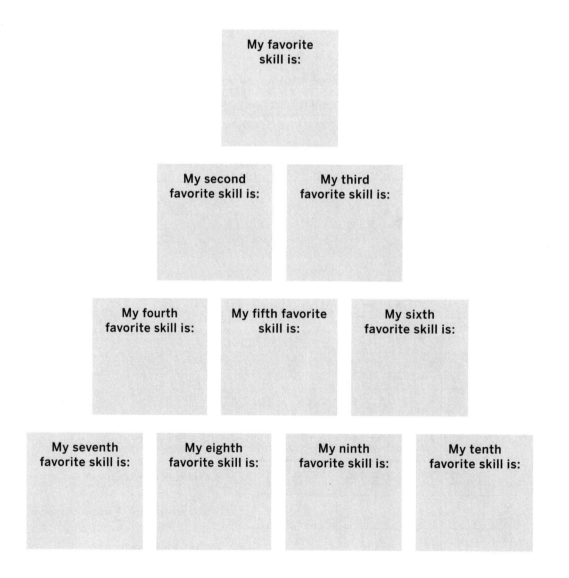

The Virtue of Depicting Your Transferable Skills in Terms of Building Blocks

Suppose it turns out that the following are your top ten favorite skills: *analyzing, teaching, researching, writing, synthesizing, entertaining, classifying, conveying warmth, leading,* and *motivating.*

If you then enter these terms onto a diagram of Building Blocks in the order of your personal priority, the top one defines the kind of job or career you are looking for. If you put "analyzing" in the top block, you might seek a job as an analyst. But if instead you move "teaching" to the top block, then you might seek a job as a teacher. And so on, with "researching," "writing," "diagnosing," and the rest. You can choose among several goals.

My favorite skill is:

My second favorite skill is:

My third favorite skill is:

My fourth favorite skill is:

My fifth favorite skill is:

My sixth favorite skill is:

My seventh favorite skill is:

My eighth favorite skill is:

My ninth favorite skill is:

My tenth favorite skill is:

MY MOST IMPORTANT TRAITS

While your stories in Worksheet #1 focused on your **skills**, let's take those same stories and see if we can find transferable **traits** that employers would value. For instance, if we go back to the "Ruffles" story, what traits can you identify in that writer? I would select patience, tenacity, compassion, and achievement orientation. Any employer would likely want someone with these traits in almost any field of employment. So go through your stories again and use the checklist on page 42 to identify the traits you exhibited. See which ones appear more than once on the grid, and make a list of your "top ten" to place on Petal 3 on page 4.

Now, let's go a little deeper.

In general, your traits describe how you deal with:

- Time and promptness
- People and emotions
- Authority and being told what to do at your job
- Supervision and being told how to do your job
- Impulse versus self-discipline, within yourself
- Initiative versus response, within yourself
- Crises or problems

If you want to know what your traits or self-management skills are, popular tests such as the MBTI (the Myers-Briggs Type Indicator) measure that sort of thing.

If you have access to the internet, there are clues about your traits or "type." Here are three sites to check out:

Myers-Briggs Foundation home page
www.myersbriggs.org
The official website of the foundation; lots of testing resources

The 16 Personality Types
www.personalitypage.com/high-level.html
A helpful site about Myers types

A CHECKLIST OF MY STRONGEST TRAITS

I am very . . .

- ☐ Accurate
- ☐ Achievement-oriented
- ☐ Adaptable
- ☐ Adept
- ☐ Adept at having fun
- ☐ Adventuresome
- ☐ Alert
- ☐ Appreciative
- ☐ Assertive
- ☐ Astute
- ☐ Authoritative
- ☐ Calm
- ☐ Cautious
- ☐ Charismatic
- ☐ Compassionate
- ☐ Competent
- ☐ Consistent
- ☐ Contagious in my enthusiasm
- ☐ Cooperative
- ☐ Courageous
- ☐ Creative
- ☐ Decisive
- ☐ Deliberate
- ☐ Dependable
- ☐ Diligent
- ☐ Diplomatic
- ☐ Discreet
- ☐ Driven

- ☐ Dynamic
- ☐ Economical
- ☐ Effective
- ☐ Energetic
- ☐ Enthusiastic
- ☐ Exceptional
- ☐ Exhaustive
- ☐ Experienced
- ☐ Expert
- ☐ Firm
- ☐ Flexible
- ☐ Human-oriented
- ☐ Impulsive
- ☐ Inclusive
- ☐ Independent
- ☐ Innovative
- ☐ Kind
- ☐ Knowledgeable
- ☐ Loyal
- ☐ Methodical
- ☐ Objective
- ☐ Open-minded
- ☐ Outgoing
- ☐ Outstanding
- ☐ Patient
- ☐ Penetrating
- ☐ Perceptive
- ☐ Persevering

- ☐ Persistent
- ☐ Pioneering
- ☐ Practical
- ☐ Professional
- ☐ Protective
- ☐ Punctual
- ☐ Quick in my work
- ☐ Rational
- ☐ Realistic
- ☐ Reliable
- ☐ Resourceful
- ☐ Responsible
- ☐ Responsive
- ☐ Safeguarding
- ☐ Self-motivated
- ☐ Self-reliant
- ☐ Sensitive
- ☐ Sophisticated
- ☐ Strong
- ☐ Supportive
- ☐ Tactful
- ☐ Tenacious
- ☐ Thorough
- ☐ Unique
- ☐ Unusual
- ☐ Versatile
- ☐ Vigorous

Working Out Your Myers-Briggs Type
www.teamtechnology.co.uk/tt/t-articl/mb-simpl.htm
An informative article about the MBTI

Another excellent test to learn more about your values is the Values-in-Action (VIA) assessment, which you can take for free online at www.authentichappiness.sas.upenn.edu/testcenter. This site, developed by the Positive Psychology Center at the University of Pennsylvania, contains several interesting and helpful work-related assessments. Try experimenting; they are free, although you have to register.

You can use your self-management skills to flesh out each of your favorite transferable skills so that you are able to describe each of your talents or skills with more than just a one-word verb or gerund.

Let's take *organizing* as our example. You tell us proudly: "I'm good at organizing." That's a fine *start* at defining your traits, but unfortunately it doesn't yet tell us much. Organizing *what*? People, as at a party? Nuts and bolts, as on a workbench? Or lots of information, as on a computer? These are three entirely different skills. The one word *organizing* doesn't tell us which one is yours.

So, please look at your favorite transferable skills or traits, and ask yourself if you want to flesh out any of them with **an object**—some kind of data/information, or some kind of people, or some kind of thing or even an idea—plus **a self-management skill or trait or style** (adverb or adjective).

Why is the trait important here? Well, "I'm good at organizing information painstakingly and logically" and "I'm good at organizing information in a flash, by intuition" are two entirely different skills. The difference between them is spelled out not in the verb, nor in the object, but in the adjectival or adverbial phrase there at the end. So, expand the definition of any of your ten favorite skills that you choose, in the fashion I have just described.

When you are face to face with a person who has the power to hire you, you want to be able to explain what makes you different from nineteen other people who can basically do the same thing that you can do. It is often the self-management skill, the trait, the adjective or adverb that will save your life, during that explanation.

Now, on to the next petal of Who You Are.

I Am a Person Who . . . Already Has (and Loves) These Particular Knowledges (or Interests)

MY FAVORITE KNOWLEDGES, INTERESTS, SUBJECTS

Goal in Filling Out This Petal: To summarize all that you have stored in your brain. Required—From your past, subjects you already know a lot about and enjoy talking about. Optional—For your future, what you would like to learn.

What You Are Looking For: Some guidance as to what field you would most enjoy working in.

Example of a Helpful Petal: Graphic design, data analysis, mathematics, how to repair a car, video games, cooking, music, principles of mechanical engineering, how to run an organization, Chinese language.

As mentioned in Petal 3, there are three things traditionally called skills: **knowledges**, as here; **functions**, also known as transferable skills; and **traits** or **self-management skills**. And as we saw there, a general rule throughout this inventory is that *knowledges are nouns; transferable skills are verbs;* and *traits are adjectives or adverbs.* If it helps knowing that, great; if not, *forget it!* Our overarching principle throughout this book is that if a generalization, metaphor, or example helps you, use it. But if it just confuses you, then ignore it!

On Petal 4 (page 4), you will eventually write your final results—your Favorite Knowledges/Fields of Interest, prioritized in the order of their importance to you.

TEN PROMPTS FOR IDENTIFYING YOUR FAVORITE KNOWLEDGES, SUBJECTS, FIELDS, OR INTERESTS (WHATEVER YOU WISH TO CALL THEM)

On a blank sheet of paper, jot down your answers to any or all of these ten prompts.

1. What are your favorite subjects or hobbies to explore (Computers? Gardening? Spanish? Law? Physics? Music?) and/or places where you like to spend your time (Museums? Medical settings? Clothing stores? Libraries? and so on)? Start a list.

2. What do you love to talk about? Ask yourself: If you were stuck on a desert island with a person who had the capacity to speak on only a few subjects, what would you pray those subjects were?

   If you were at a get-together, talking with someone who was covering two of your favorite subjects at once, which way would you hope the conversation would go? Toward which subject?

   If you could talk about something with some world expert, all day long, day after day, what would that subject or field of interest be? Add any ideas that these questions spark in you to your list.

3. What magazine articles or blogs do you love to read? You get really interested when you see a blog that deals with . . . what subject? Add any ideas to your list.

4. What newspaper articles do you love to read or podcasts do you like to listen to? You get really interested when you see a TV news report that deals with . . . what subject? Add any ideas to your list.

5. If you're browsing in a bookstore, what sections do you tend to gravitate toward? What subjects there do you find really fascinating? Add any ideas to your list.

6. What sites on the internet do you tend to gravitate toward? What subjects do these sites deal with? Do any of these really fascinate you? Add any ideas to your list.

7. What television shows do you tend to watch? What do you enjoy about them? Add any ideas to your list.

8. When you look at a catalog of courses that you could take in your town or city (or on the internet), which subjects really interest you? Add any ideas to your list.

9. If you could write a book, and it wasn't about your own life or somebody else's, what would be the subject of the book? Add it to your list.

10. There are moments, in most of our lives, when we are so engrossed in a task that we lose all track of time. (Someone has to remind us that it's time for supper, or whatever.) If this ever happens to you, what task, what subject, so absorbs your attention that you lose all track of time? Add it to your list.

PETAL 4, WORKSHEET #2

CHART OF ALL THE THINGS YOU'VE LEARNED: THE FISHERMAN'S NET

The chart on the facing page is like **a commercial fisherman's net**, which you want to cast into the sea to capture the largest haul of fish possible, and only later do you pick out the best from your haul. But we start *big*.

How to fill out this chart? Well, that's your choice. You may want to fill this out at one sitting, or you may prefer to keep it in your pocket and jot down anything that occurs to you over a period of two or three weeks: every bright idea, every hunch, every remembered dream, every intuition that pops up. *This is an important petal—very important—as it may help you unearth a field or fields where you would really like to work. So it's worth spending some time on.*

Now, following are some hints to help you fill in the first three parts of your Fisherman's Net.

THE FISHERMAN'S NET

Notes About the Knowledges, Subjects, or Interests I've Picked Up Thus Far in My Life

1. What I know from my previous jobs:	2. What I know about or picked up, outside of work:

3. What fields, careers, or industries sound interesting to me:	4. Any other hunches, bright ideas, great ideas, and the like that occur to me:

Part 1. What You Know from Your Previous Jobs

If you've been out there in the world of work for some time, you've probably learned a lot of things that you now just take for granted. "Of course I know that!" But such knowledges may be important, in and of themselves, or they may point you to something important down the line. So don't be afraid to really get detailed.

Examples: It can be work such as bookkeeping, handling applications, credit collection of overdue accounts, hiring, international business, management, marketing, sales, merchandising, packaging, policy development, problem solving, troubleshooting, public speaking, recruiting, conference planning, systems analysis, the culture of other countries, other languages, government contract procedures, and so on.

Think of each job you've ever held and then jot down any system or procedure that you learned there. For example "Worked in a warehouse: learned how to use a forklift and crane, inventory control, logistics automation software, warehouse management systems, teamwork principles, and how to supervise employees."

Or "Worked at a fast food place: learned how to prepare and serve food, how to wait on customers, how to make change, how to deal with complaints, how to train new employees."

Part 2. What You Know Outside of Work

Jot down any bodies of knowledge that you picked up on your own just because the subject fascinated you, such as antiques, gardening, cooking, budgeting, decorating, photography, crafts, spirituality, sports, camping, travel, repairing things, flea markets, scrapbooking, sewing, art appreciation at museums, how to run or work in a volunteer organization, and so on.

- Also think of anything you learned in high school (or college) that you prize knowing today: keyboarding, Chinese, accounting, geography?

- Think of anything you learned at training seminars, workshops, conferences, and so on, possibly in connection with a job you had at the time. Or something you decided to attend on your own.

- Think of anything you've studied at home, via online courses, mobile apps, podcasts, YouTube videos, PBS television or programs.

- Think of anything you learned out there in the world, such as *how to assemble a flash mob, how to organize a protest, how to fund-raise for a particular cause, how to run a marathon, how to repair a toilet.*

Is this knowledge important to you? Figure that out later; for now, your goal is to just cast as wide a net as possible.

Part 3. What Fields, Careers, or Industries Sound Interesting to You

Broadly speaking, the workplace consists of the following six fields: *agriculture, manufacturing, information, technology, finance,* and *services.* Any ideas about which of these six is most attractive to you, right off the bat? If so, jot your answer down in the third section of the chart.

To drill down further into these six, your best bet is the government's O*NET OnLine (www.onetonline.org).

O*NET OnLine has various lists of **career clusters** or **industries** or **job families**. The following list is a mashup of these. Please read over it and copy down any of these that you want to explore further. Multiple choices are preferred here, in order to have alternatives and, therefore, hope.

- ☐ Accommodation and Food Services
- ☐ Administrative and Support Services
- ☐ Agriculture, Food, and Natural Resources
- ☐ Architecture, Engineering, and Construction
- ☐ Arts, Audio/Video Technology, and Communications
- ☐ Business, Operations, Management, and Administration
- ☐ Community and Social Services
- ☐ Computer and Mathematical
- ☐ Design, Entertainment, Sports, and Media
- ☐ Distribution and Logistics
- ☐ Education, Training, and Library
- ☐ Entertainment and Recreation
- ☐ Farming, Forestry, Fishing, and Hunting
- ☐ Finance and Insurance
- ☐ Food Preparation and Serving
- ☐ Government and Public Administration
- ☐ Green Industries or Jobs
- ☐ Health Care, Health Science, and Social Assistance
- ☐ Hospitality and Tourism
- ☐ Human Services
- ☐ Information and Information Technology
- ☐ Law, Public Safety, Corrections, and Security

- ☐ Life, Physical, and Social Sciences
- ☐ Management of Companies and Enterprises
- ☐ Manufacturing
- ☐ Marketing, Sales, and Service
- ☐ Military Related
- ☐ Mining, Quarrying, and Oil and Gas Extraction
- ☐ Personal Care and Service
- ☐ Production
- ☐ Professional, Scientific, and Technical Services
- ☐ Protective Services
- ☐ Real Estate, Rental, and Leasing
- ☐ Religion, Faith, and Related
- ☐ Retail Trade, Sales, and Related
- ☐ Science, Technology, Engineering, and Mathematics
- ☐ Self-Employment
- ☐ Transportation, Warehousing, and Material Moving
- ☐ Utilities

With the O*NET OnLine, when you have chosen any items on this list, drop-down menus allow you to go deeper into each *career cluster, industry,* or *job family* that you have checked off. These drill down to **career pathways** and then down further to **individual occupations**, and still further to **tasks**, **tools**, **technologies**, **knowledges**, **skills**, **abilities**, **work activities**, **education**, **interests**, **work styles**, **work values**, **related occupations**, and **salary**.

Remember: Jobs, industries, and careers are *mortal*; they are born, they grow, they mature, they flourish, then decline and ultimately die. Sometimes it takes centuries, sometimes merely decades, sometimes even less time than that. But eventually most jobs, industries, and careers are mortal.

We are mortal. So are jobs. Understand that truth, and you will avoid a life of bitterness and blame. In today's world, you must *always* have a plan B up your sleeve.

PRIORITIZING YOUR KNOWLEDGES: FAVORITE SUBJECTS MATRIX

Okay, now you've completed Worksheet #2. You've cast as wide a commercial fisherman's net—so to speak—as possible, using Worksheet #1 and Worksheet #2 for this Petal. What now?

Well, it's time to pick the best of your haul, as we indicated earlier. Time to look it all over and decide which knowledges, subjects, or interests are your favorites. Time for prioritizing. We're going to use a different kind of prioritizing aid here; not our familiar Grid, but four boxes/compartments/"bins" along the axes of Expertise and Enthusiasm. In other words, a matrix.

Before you begin, copy the matrix on the facing page onto a much larger piece of paper.

Then copy everything—*everything*—you have written down on Worksheet #1 (Ten Prompts) and Worksheet #2 (the Chart) and decide which of the four bins it belongs in, as you weigh your expertise (or lack of it) and your enthusiasm (or lack of it) with that particular subject or knowledge.

(You don't have to copy anything into bin #4 if you don't want to—except if you want it to stand there, filled with subjects and knowledges that you don't care about, as a cautionary tale. I'll state the obvious: Any knowledge that you have neither any expertise in nor any enthusiasm for is a knowledge you will want to avoid at all costs in a future job, if it's up to you. And it is.)

Once you have finished copying the knowledge from Worksheets #1 and #2 into these bins, go back and study only what you put into bin #1: *High Expertise, High Enthusiasm.* Copy what you consider to be your top four or five favorites from that bin—*use a Prioritizing Grid if you need to*—and maybe, just maybe, one item from bin #2, and put them on Petal 4, found on page 4.

Your Favorite Knowledges, Subjects, Fields, Interests—whatever you want to call them—is done. Now you're ready to move on, to consider the fifth side of Who You Are.

YOUR FAVORITE SUBJECTS MATRIX

HIGH	**3.** Subjects for Which You Have Little Enthusiasm but in Which You Have Lots of Expertise	**1.** Subjects for Which You Have Lots of Enthusiasm and in Which You Have Lots of Expertise BINGO!
	4. Subjects for Which You Have Little Enthusiasm and in Which You Have Little Expertise	**2.** Subjects for Which You Have Lots of Enthusiasm but in Which You Have Little Expertise
LOW		

Expertise

LOW → HIGH

Enthusiasm

I Am a Person Who . . . Prefers a Certain Level of Salary and Responsibility

MY PREFERRED LEVEL OF SALARY AND RESPONSIBILITY

Goal in Filling Out This Petal: To gain a realistic picture of how much money you will need to earn, or want to earn, at whatever job you find.

What You Are Looking For: A range, because most employers are thinking in terms of a range, too. When you negotiate salary—as you will almost certainly have to, if the employer is of any significant size—you want to get the best outcome for your needs.

Form of the Entries on Your Petal: Total dollars needed, weekly, monthly, or annually. Stated in thousands (symbol: K).

Example of a Helpful Petal: $75K to $85K (good because it's a range, is realistic based on your research into the career field, and is justifiable based on your levels of experience and education).

A Crash Course in Money

Money is important. Or else we're reduced to bartering for our food, clothing, and shelter. So, when we're out of work, unless we have huge amounts of money in our savings account or investments, we are inevitably thinking: *What am I going to do so that I have enough money to put food on the table, clothes on my back, and a roof over our heads for myself—and for my family or partner (if I have one)?*

Happiness is important, too. So we may find ourselves thinking: *How much do I really need to be earning, for me to be truly happy with my life?*

Are these two worries—money and happiness—related? Can money buy happiness?

Partly, it turns out. Partly. A study published in 2010, of the responses of 450,000 people in the US to a daily survey, found that the less money they made, the more unhappy they tended to be, day after day. No surprise there. And, obviously, the more money they made, measured in terms of percentage improvement, the happier they tended to be, *as measured by the frequency and intensity of moments of smiling, laughter, affection, and joy all day long, versus moments of sadness, worry, and stress.*

So money does buy happiness. *But only up to a point.* That point was found to be around $75,000 annual income, with a satiation point at $95,000. If people made more money annually than $75,000, it of course further improved their *satisfaction* with how their life was going, but it did not increase their *happiness.* Above $75,000, they started to report reduced ability to spend time with people they liked, to enjoy leisure, and to savor small pleasures. Happiness depends on things like that, and on other factors, too: good health; a loving relationship; loving friends; and a feeling of competence—gaining mastery, respect, praise, or even love because we are really good at what we do.

So this petal cannot be filled out all by itself. It is inextricably tied to the other petals—most particularly, to what you love to do and where you love to do it.

Still, salary is something you must think about ahead of time, when you're contemplating your ideal job or career. Responsibility goes hand in hand with salary, of course. So here are a few of questions you should be asking yourself.

1. At what level would you like to work, in your ideal job?

Level is a matter of how much responsibility you want in an organization:

- Boss or CEO (this may mean you'll have to form your own business)
- Manager or someone under the boss who carries out orders
- The head of a team

- A member of a team of equals
- One who works in tandem with one other partner
- One who works alone, as an employee, a consultant to an organization, or a one-person business

Think carefully about your answer, talk it over with your friends or family, then enter a two- or three-word summary of your answer (for now) on Petal 6, the Preferred Salary and Level of Responsibility, of your Flower Diagram, page 5.

2. What salary would you like to be aiming for?

It's a mistake to hyperfocus on one number during salary negotiation. Here you have to think in terms of a range, not a single figure. One way to do this is to think of your minimum or maximum desired.

Minimum is what you would need to make to just barely get by. And incidentally, you do need to know this *before* you go in for a job interview with anyone (or before you form your own business, and need to know how much profit you must make, just to survive). You can't survive on a negative income stream.

Maximum could be any astronomical figure you can think of, but it is more useful here to put down the salary you realistically think you could make, with your present competency and experience, were you working for a real, *but generous*, boss. (If this maximum figure is still depressingly low, then put down the salary you would like to be making five years from now.)

3. What benefits package would you like to aim for?

Keep in mind that a better benefits package than you currently have can offset a slightly lower salary offer than you would like. Once again, you must know what's most important about your compensation. Even though there are copays and other costs associated with benefits, a strong benefits package can increase your overall compensation by as much as 30 percent beyond your salary. Some possible benefits include:

- Healthcare (medical, dental, vision)
- Bonuses
- Disability insurance (long-term and short-term)
- Free meals
- Retirement (401[k] or 403[b]) or pension
- Sick/parental leave
- Vacation time/holidays

- Child care (free or low-cost)
- Stock options
- Tuition reimbursement for self or children
- Work-from-home flexibility

Are any of these benefits imperative for you? Which ones are unnecessary? Knowing what you need in terms of benefits can help you greatly in your salary negotiations.

PETAL 5, WORKSHEET #1
A BUDGET: KEEPING TRACK OF HOW MUCH YOU DO SPEND AND HOW MUCH YOU'D LIKE TO SPEND

We all think we know how much money we need to earn. But one of the best ways to really know is by making a budget. On the next page you will find a simple guide to the categories you will need to think about. Figure out what you think you will need *monthly* in each category. And if you see any categories missing, do not hesitate to add them.

One of the best ways to start determining your necessary income is to keep track of how you actually spend your money. You can just jot down notes at the end of each day. Lots of apps make this task much easier. For example, there is Spending Tracker, Pocket Expense, Goodbudget, and, for all those who want to sync with their bank accounts, Mint.com.

The good news: all are simple, and all are free.

Once you figure out what you *actually* spend, you'll be much better able to lay out a realistic budget of what you *want* to spend.

In any event, by hook or by crook, once you have your monthly budget, it's time to do some math. Fill out your monthly expenses chart on the next two pages.

Multiply the total amount you need each month by 12, to get the yearly figure.

Divide the yearly figure by 2,000, and you will be reasonably near the *minimum* hourly wage that you need. Thus, if you need $3,333 per month, multiplied by 12 that's $40,000 a year, and then divided by 2,000, that's $20 an hour.

You will also want to put down the *maximum* salary you would like to make (dream, dream, dream). Once you are done, enter both salary figures—minimum and maximum—and any notes you want to add, such as to justify the maximum (you may also want to add any non-monetary rewards you seek from the Optional Exercise on page 52) and add all of this on Petal 6, the Preferred Salary and Level of Responsibility petal, found on page 5.

Housing

Rent or mortgage payments . . . . $_____

Electricity/gas. . . . . $_____

Water . . . . $_____

Phone/internet. . . . . $_____

Garbage removal . . . . $_____

Cleaning, maintenance, repairs . . . . $_____

Food

What you spend at the supermarket

and/or farmers' market . . . . $_____

Eating out . . . . $_____

Clothing

Purchase of new or used clothing . . . . $_____

Cleaning, dry cleaning, laundry . . . . $_____

Automobile/transportation

Car payments . . . . $_____

Gas . . . . $_____

Repairs. . . . . $_____

Public transportation (bus, train, plane). . . . . $_____

Insurance

Car . . . . $_____

Medical or health care . . . . $_____

House and personal possessions. . . . . $_____

Life . . . . $_____

Medical expenses

Doctors' visits. . . . . $_____

Prescriptions. . . . . $_____

Fitness costs . . . . $_____

Support for other family members

Child care costs (if you have children) . . . . $_____

Child support (if you're paying that). . . . . $_____

Support for your parents (if you're helping out). $_____

Charity giving/tithe (to help others) . . . . $_____

School/learning

Children's costs (if you have children in school) . . . . $_____

Your learning costs (adult education, job-hunting classes) . . . . $_____

Pet care (if you have pets) . . . . $_____

Bills and debts (usual monthly payments)

    Credit cards . . . . $_____

    Other obligations you pay off monthly. . . . . $_____

Taxes

    Federal (annual return, divided by twelve months) . . . . $_____

    State (annual, divided by twelve months) . . . . $_____

    Local/property (annual, divided by twelve months). . . . . $_____

    Tax help (if you ever use an accountant, or

        pay a friend to help you with taxes) . . . . $_____

Savings (what you currently deposit each month) . . . . $_____

Retirement Contributions . . . . $_____

Amusement/discretionary spending

    Movies, Netflix, other. . . . . $_____

    Other entertainment. . . . . $_____

    Reading: newspapers, magazines, books . . . . $_____

    Gifts (birthdays, holidays, anniversaries) . . . . $_____

    Vacations. . . . . $_____

Total Amount You Need Each Month . . . . $_____

AN OPTIONAL EXERCISE: OTHER REWARDS BESIDES MONEY

If you do check off things on this list, arrange your answers in order of importance to you, and then add them to the petal.

You may wish to put down other rewards, besides money, that you would hope for from your next job or career. These might be:

- ☐ A chance to be creative
- ☐ A chance to exercise leadership
- ☐ A chance to help others
- ☐ A chance to make decisions
- ☐ A chance to use your expertise
- ☐ A diverse work environment
- ☐ Adventure
- ☐ Challenge
- ☐ Fame
- ☐ Influence
- ☐ Intellectual stimulation
- ☐ Popularity
- ☐ Power
- ☐ Respect
- ☐ Other

Now, on to the sixth side of Who You Are.

I Am a Person Who . . . Prefers Certain Places to Live

MY PREFERRED PLACE(S) TO LIVE

Goal in Filling Out This Petal: To define in what part of the country or the world you would most like to work and live, and would be happiest, if you ever have a choice. Also to resolve any conflict (should it arise) between you and your partner as to where you want to live after you retire or make your next career move.

What You Are Looking For: Forming a clearer picture about what you hope for in life, now or later. Now, if you're able to move and want to make a wise decision as to where. Later, if you're currently tied down to a particular place because "I need to be near my kids or my ailing parents," or whatever, in which case this becomes a planning for the future: retirement, or earlier. It's important to think about the future now, because an opportunity may come along when you least expect it, and you might pass right by it, unless you've given it some thought and instantly recognize it.

Form of the Entries on Your Petal: You can stay general (city, suburbs, rural, up in the mountains, on the coast, or overseas) or you can get very specific if you're really ready to move, naming names and places—as this exercise will teach you to do.

Example of a Helpful Petal: First preference, San Francisco; second preference, Honolulu; third preference, New York City.

A CHART: WHAT I LIKED OR DISLIKED ABOUT PLACES I HAVE LIVED

This exercise will help you identify the geographical qualities you most prefer. If you are doing this exercise with a partner, make a copy for them, too, so that each of you is working on a clean copy of your own and can follow these instructions independently. Ask your partner to complete the same list with the first four columns, and have them create a page with the list of possible locations that fit their characteristics.

Now, to fill out this chart:

Column 1. List all the places where you have ever lived.

Column 2. List all the factors you disliked about each place.

Column 3. Review column 2, your list of negative factors, and in column 3 try to list each one's opposite (or near opposite). For example, "the sun never shone there" would, in column 3, be turned into "mostly sunny, all year-round." It will not always be the exact opposite. The negative factor "rains all the time" does not necessarily translate into the positive "sunny all the time." It might be something like "sunny at least 200 days a year." It's your call. Keep going until every negative factor in column 2 has an opposite, positive factor, in column 3.

(At this point, you don't really need column 1. Its purpose was to jog your memory.)

Column 4. List the positive factors in column 3, from most important to you to least important. For example, if you were looking at and trying to name a new town, city, or place where you could be happy and flourish, what is the first thing you would look for? Would it be good weather? Lack of crime? Good schools? Access to cultural opportunities, such as music, art, museums, or whatever? Inexpensive housing? Rank all the factors in column 4. If you need an organizing tool, use the ten-item Prioritizing Grid on the page 66.

Show and tell. Once you're done, on a fresh blank sheet of paper list those top ten factors, in order of importance to you. For the next ten days, show it to everyone you meet and ask them: "Can you think of any place that has all ten of these factors, or at least the top five?" Jot down any and all of their suggestions on the back of the paper. When the ten days are up, look at the back of that sheet and circle the three places that seem the most interesting to you. If there is only a partial overlap between your dream factors and the places your friends and acquaintances can come up with, *make sure the overlap is in the factors that count the most.* Google can help, too. Try searching "cities with lowest crime rates" or "best places for sunshine in US" and see what shows up. Just keep in mind that some of those lists are not neutral. They may be influenced by a sponsor or whatever group produced it, such as a tourism company or the local chamber of commerce.

MY GEOGRAPHICAL PREFERENCES
Decision Making for Just You

COLUMN 1	COLUMN 2	COLUMN 3
Names of Places I Have Lived	**From the Past: Negatives**	**Translating the Negatives into Positives**
	Factors I Disliked and Still Dislike About Any Place	Factors I Liked and Still Like About Any Place

MY GEOGRAPHICAL PREFERENCES
Decision Making for Just You

COLUMN 4	COLUMN 5
Ranking of My Positives	Places That Fit These Criteria
1.	
2.	
3.	
4.	
5.	
6.	
7.	
8.	
9.	
10.	

OUR GEOGRAPHICAL PREFERENCES
Decision Making for You and a Partner

COLUMN 6	COLUMN 7	COLUMN 8
Ranking of Their Partner's Preferences	**Combining Our Two Lists (columns 4 & 6)**	**Places That Fit These Criteria**
a.	1.	
	a.	
b.	2.	
	b.	
c.	3.	
	c.	
d.	4.	
	d.	
e.	5.	
	e.	
f.	6.	
	f.	
g.	7.	
	g.	
h.	8.	
	h.	
i.	9.	
	i.	
j.	10.	
	j.	

PRIORITIZING GRID

FOR 10 ITEMS OR FEWER

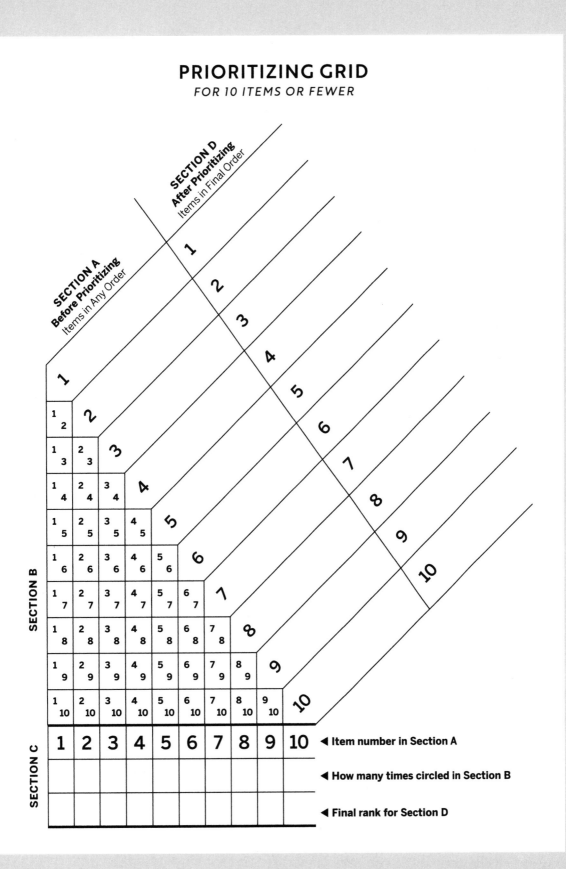

◀ Item number in Section A

◀ How many times circled in Section B

◀ Final rank for Section D

Column 5. You now have some locations you will want to find out more about, so that you can eventually figure out which would be your absolute favorite place to live, and your second, and your third, as backups. Enter those top three places in column 5, then copy these, plus your top five geographical factors, onto Petal 6, Preferred Places to Live, on the Flower Diagram on pages 4–5.

Column 6. *If you're working with a partner,* it's time to compare your lists. In column 6, place your partner's top choices.

Column 7. Alternate writing your partner's and your ranked choices

Did you find any places where your lists agree or at least complement each other? Did you select the same cities? Same general geographic areas?

Column 8. Try coming up with a prioritized list you both can agree on and list those places (or criteria) and place them here.

By looking at columns 7 and 8, you will now know the key elements that are important to each of you and both of you. You will also have a list of places that might work for each of you—and both of you. Review these columns together and start developing your top three places that you both would feel comfortable about.

Finally, both of you should put the names of those top three places, plus your top five geographical factors, onto Petal 6, the Preferred Places to Live petal, on both of your Flower Diagrams, pages 4–5.

Conclusion for Petal 6

Does all this seem like just too much work? Well, there are a few options you *may* want to try. The first is a website called Teleport (teleport.org). See if it helps you at all. One reader said, about a similar site, "I found it useful. It showed me towns I'd never thought about." Consider vacationing in your top choice locations. Spend at least a week and pretend you live there. Talk to a real estate agent or look at where apartments are available in which neighborhoods. Take time to visit grocery stores, shops, and restaurants.

The third alternative: Have everyone in the house throw darts at a map (of the US or wherever) that you've pinned to a dartboard. See what place the most darts came near. (One family did this after they couldn't agree on any location. For them it came out Denver. So, Denver it was!)

I Am a Person Who . . . Has a Certain Goal, Mission, or Purpose in Life

MY MSSION OR SENSE OF PURPOSE FOR MY LIFE

Goal in Filling Out This Petal: To know the moral compass or spiritual values by which you want to guide your life, or the overall goals that inspire you.

What You Are Looking For: Some definition of your overall goals, mission, and/ or purpose of your life. This may help you pick out the kinds of organizations or companies you'd like to work for, if you find ones that are serving the same mission as yours.

Form of the Entries on Your Petal: A description of what sphere of life you want to make better, with some attending details.

Example of a Helpful Petal: My purpose in life is to help others through my teaching. I want there to be more knowledge, more compassion, more forgiveness, in those I have worked or lived with, because I have taught them.

You need to dream about the broad outcome of your life and not just this year's job search. What kind of footprint do you want to leave on this Earth, after your journey here is done? Figure that out and you're well on your way to defining your life as having purpose and a mission. As John Holland famously said, "We need to look further down the road than just headlight range at night." The road is the road of life.

DIAGRAM: THE NINE SPHERES OF PURPOSE OR MISSION

Generally speaking, purpose can be broken down into nine spheres, corresponding to our nature. As you look these over in the diagram on page 70, which one appeals to *you* the most? Time for some hard thinking (ouch!). So study this diagram *slowly*. Take time to ponder and think. Consider circling the elements that are most important to you.

Now let's look at these in more detail. Consider these as spheres, environments, or arenas in which you like to play.

1. **The Sphere of the Senses.** When you have finished your life on Earth, do you want there to be more beauty in the world because you were here? If so, what kind of beauty entrances you? Is it art, music, flowers, photography, painting, staging, crafts, clothing, jewelry, or something else? If this is your main purpose in life, then write one paragraph about it.

2. **The Sphere of the Body.** When you have finished your life on Earth, do you want there to be more wholeness, fitness, or health in the world, more healing of the body's wounds, more feeding of the hungry and clothing of the poor, because you were here? What issue in particular? If this is your main purpose in life, then write one paragraph about it.

3. **The Sphere of Our Possessions.** Is your major concern the often false love of possessions in this world? When you have finished your life on Earth, do you want there to be better stewardship of what we possess—as individuals, as a community, as a nation—in the world, because you were here? Do you want to see simplicity, quality (rather than quantity), and a broader emphasis on the word "enough," rather than on the words "more, more"? If so, in what areas of human life in particular? If this is your main purpose in life, then write one paragraph about it.

4. **The Sphere of the Will or Conscience.** When you have finished your life on Earth, do you want there to be more morality, more justice, more righteousness, more honesty in the world, because you were here? In what areas of human life or history, in particular? And in what geographical area? If this is your main purpose in life, then write one paragraph about it.

5. **The Sphere of the Heart.** When you have finished your life on Earth, do you want there to be more love and compassion in the world, because you were here? Love or compassion for whom? Or for what? If this is your main purpose in life, then write one paragraph about it.

6. **The Sphere of Entertainment.** When you have finished your life on Earth, do you want there to be more lightening of people's loads, more giving them perspective, more helping them to forget their cares for a spell; do you want there to be more laughter in the world, and joy, because you were here? If so, what particular kind of entertainment do you want to contribute to the world? If this is your main purpose in life, then write one paragraph about it.

7. **The Sphere of the Earth.** Is the planet on which we stand your major concern? When you have finished your life on Earth, do you want there to be better protection of this fragile planet, more exploration of the world or the universe—exploration, not exploitation— more dealing with its problems and its energy, because you were here? If so, which problems or challenges, in particular, draw your heart and soul? If this is your main purpose in life, then write one paragraph about it.

8. **The Sphere of the Spirit.** When you have finished your life on Earth, do you want there to be more spirituality in the world, more faith, more compassion, more forgiveness, more love for a higher power and the human family in all its diversity, because you were here? If so, with what ages, or people, or with what parts of human life? If this is your main purpose in life, then write one paragraph about it.

9. **The Sphere of the Mind.** When you have finished your life on Earth, do you want there to be more knowledge, truth, or clarity in the world, because you were here? Knowledge, truth, or clarity concerning what in particular? If this is your main purpose in life, then write one paragraph about it.

In sum, remember that all of these are worthwhile purposes and missions, all of these are necessary and needed in this world. The question is, Which one in particular draws you to it *the most?* Which one do you most want to lend your brain, your energies, your skills and gifts, your life, to serve while you are here on this Earth?

When you are done, enter a summary paragraph of what you have decided your purpose is on Petal 7, your Goal, Mission, or Purpose in Life, on page 5.

THE PURPOSE FOR MY LIFE:
I WANT THERE TO BE MORE . . . (CHOOSE)

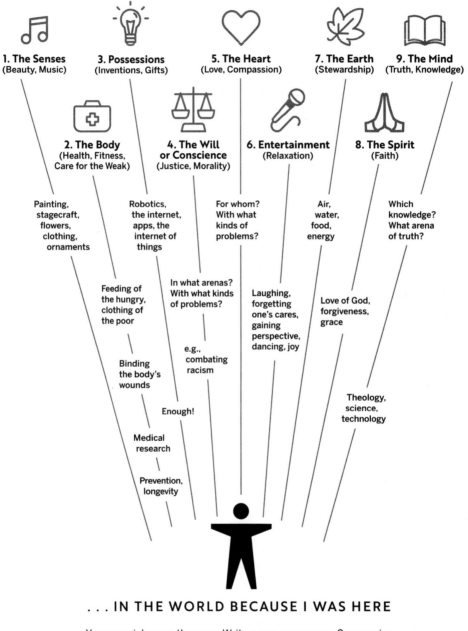

1. The Senses
(Beauty, Music)

3. Possessions
(Inventions, Gifts)

5. The Heart
(Love, Compassion)

7. The Earth
(Stewardship)

9. The Mind
(Truth, Knowledge)

2. The Body
(Health, Fitness,
Care for the Weak)

**4. The Will
or Conscience**
(Justice, Morality)

6. Entertainment
(Relaxation)

8. The Spirit
(Faith)

Painting,
stagecraft,
flowers,
clothing,
ornaments

Robotics,
the internet,
apps, the
internet of
things

For whom?
With what
kinds of
problems?

Air,
water,
food,
energy

Which
knowledge?
What arena
of truth?

Feeding of
the hungry,
clothing of
the poor

In what arenas?
With what kinds
of problems?

Laughing,
forgetting
one's cares,
gaining
perspective,
dancing, joy

Love of God,
forgiveness,
grace

Binding
the body's
wounds

e.g.,
combating
racism

Enough!

Theology,
science,
technology

Medical
research

Prevention,
longevity

. . . IN THE WORLD BECAUSE I WAS HERE

You may pick more than one. Write a one-page essay. Summarize
it on the Goal, Mission, or Purpose in Life petal, page 5.

ESSAY: YOUR PHILOSOPHY ABOUT LIFE

There are two challenges you may run into with this petal.

First Challenge: You just come up empty on this exercise, despite hard thinking. No harm done. If you want an answer, just keep the question on the back burner of your mind; eventually, some insight is going to break through—tomorrow, next week, next month, or a year from now. Be patient with yourself.

Second Challenge: This subject doesn't interest you at all. Okay. Then instead of writing a statement of purpose or mission for your life, you can instead write a statement outlining what you think about *life*: why are we here, why are *you* here, and so on. This is often called your philosophy of life.

In writing a philosophy of life, aim for it to run no more than two pages, single spaced, and it can be less. It should address whichever of the following elements you think are most important; pick and choose. You do *not* have to write about all of them. In most cases, you will need two or three sentences about each element you choose to comment on.

- **Beauty:** what kind of beauty stirs you; the function of beauty in the world
- **Behavior:** how you think we should behave in this world
- **Beliefs:** your strongest beliefs
- **Celebration:** how you like to play or celebrate
- **Choice:** its nature and importance to you
- **Community:** your concept of belonging to each other; what you think is our responsibility to each other
- **Compassion:** how you demonstrate it to yourself and others
- **Confusion:** how you live with it and deal with it
- **Death:** what you think about it and what you think happens after it
- **Events:** what you think makes things happen; how you explain why they happen
- **Free will:** whether our lives are "predetermined" or we have free will
- **Happiness:** what makes for the truest human happiness
- **Heroes:** who yours are, and why
- **Humanity:** what you think is important about being human, what you think is our function
- **Love:** what you think about its nature and importance, along with all its related words—compassion, forgiveness, grace

- **Moral issues:** which ones you believe are the most important for us to pay attention to, wrestle with, help solve
- **Paradox:** your attitude toward its presence in life
- **Purpose:** why we are here, what life is all about
- **Reality:** what you think is its nature and components
- **Self:** whether physical self is the limit of your being; what trust-in-self means
- **Spirituality:** its place in human life, how we should treat it
- **Stewardship:** what we should do with the gifts we have been given
- **Truth:** what you think about it; which truths are most important
- **Uniqueness:** what you think makes each of us unique
- **Universe:** your concept of what holds the universe together— a supreme being or other force
- **Values:** what you think about humanity, what you think about the world, ranked by what matters most (to you)

When you are done writing, put a summary paragraph on or near Petal 7, your Goal, Mission, or Purpose in Life, on page 5. And you're done!

CONCLUSION

It's hard to argue with success, and the millions of copies sold of this book are a testament to its value in the job search process. A system like this only works, though, if you do the work and follow it. The Parachute System requires a commitment of both time and energy, but there's also a spark of magic involved. And that magic is you and what you bring to the process.

- Were you able to create your Flower Exercise, and did you gain new insights or receive more clarity on yourself and your plans?

- Did you discover new career fields to pursue, put the internet to work in your search, or create new or better stories for your interviews or conversations?

- Even better, did using this system lead you to a new job, a better job, or whatever you were seeing?

A Light Bulb Goes On

For some of you there will be a big *Aha!* as you look at your Flower Diagram. A light bulb will go on, over your head, and you will say, "My goodness, I see *exactly* what sort of career this points me to." This happens particularly with intuitive people.

If you are one of those intuitive people, I say, "Good for you!" Just two gentle warnings, if I may.

Don't prematurely close out *other* possibilities.

And *don't* say to yourself: "Well, I see what it is that I would die to be able to do, but I *know* there is no job in the world like that, that *I* would be able to get." Dear friend, you don't know any such thing. You haven't done your research yet. Of course, it is always possible that when you've completed all that research, and conducted your search, you still may not be able to find *all* that you want—down to the last detail. But you'd be surprised at how much of your dream you may be able to find.

Other Possibility, You Look at Your Flower Diagram and . . . a Light Bulb *Doesn't* Go On

In contrast to what I just said, many of you will look at your completed Flower Diagram, and you won't have *a clue* as to what job or career it points to. *Soooo*, we need a "fallback" strategy.

First, write down on one piece of paper your top five favorite Transferable Skills and your top three favorite Knowledges from your Flower, and then ask at least five friends, family members, and professionals you know to offer what job titles and job fields come to mind. Then, approach contacts in those fields for Informational Interviews. During Informational Interviewing, you want to talk to people who are actually doing the work you think you'd love to do. Why? In effect, you are mentally *trying on jobs* to see if they fit you.

Once you discover places you'd like to work for, do some preliminary research on them before you approach them for an interview.

And remember, always send a thank-you note to anyone who helps you along the way.

Need More Help?

This should get you started toward finding your dream job, with the Flower as your guide. For more information on job-hunting, I invite you to consult with the book for which this workbook is a companion: *What Color Is Your Parachute? Your Guide to a Lifetime of Meaningful Work and Career Success*, by yours truly.

Don't just drop your Flower at this point. Be persistent, be thorough, and don't give up just because your Flower doesn't immediately point you toward the next step. Keep showing your Flower to anyone and everyone, and ask what suggestions they can make. This is your life you're working on, your *Life*. Make it glorious.

ABOUT THE AUTHORS

DICK BOLLES—more formally known as Richard Nelson Bolles—led the career development field for more than four decades. He was featured in the *New York Times, Time, Bloomberg BusinessWeek, Fortune, Money, Fast Company, The Economist,* and *Publishers Weekly,* and appeared on the *Today* show, CNN, CBS, ABC, PBS, and other popular media. Bolles keynoted hundreds of conferences, including the American Society for Training and Development and the National Career Development Association. A member of Mensa, the Society for Human Resource Management, and the National Résumé Writers' Association, he was considered "the most recognized job-hunting authority on the planet" (*San Francisco Chronicle*) and "America's top career expert" (*AARP*).

Time magazine chose *What Color Is Your Parachute?* as one of the hundred best nonfiction books written since 1923. The Library of Congress chose it as one of twenty-five books down through history that have shaped people's lives. It appeared on the *New York Times* bestseller list for more than five years. The book has sold ten million copies, to date, and has been translated into twenty languages and used in twenty-six countries.

Bolles was trained in chemical engineering at Massachusetts Institute of Technology, and earned a bachelor's degree cum laude in physics from Harvard University, a master's in sacred theology from The General Theological Seminary of the Episcopal Church in New York City, and three honorary doctorates. He passed away in 2017 at age ninety after a lifetime of service to job-hunters across the world.

KATHARINE BROOKS, EdD—is an award-winning career counselor and coach who is currently the Evans Family executive director of the Career Center for Vanderbilt University. She is a licensed professional counselor, a nationally certified counselor, and a board-certified coach. Previously, she had been the executive director of the Office of Personal and Career Development at Wake Forest University and director of Career Services for the College of Liberal Arts at the University of Texas at Austin. She is the author of *You Majored in What?: Designing Your Path from College to Career, What Color is Your Parachute? for College,* and writes a blog, "Career Transitions," for *Psychology Today.*

THE COMPLETE PARACHUTE LIBRARY

A quick guide to the job search, for when time is of the essence.

A slender guide to writing a winning resume and cover letter that will help you land interviews.

A slender guide to help you ace the interview and land your dream job.

A guide to help students zero in on the perfect major or career.

How to choose a major, create a four-year plan, and make the most of your college experience.

Practical tools and exercises for a prosperous retirement.

Learn to use the internet effectively for all aspects of your job-hunt.

A complete guide for practicing or aspiring career counselors.

Visit parachutebook.com and JobHuntersBible.com

Available from Ten Speed Press wherever books are sold.
www.tenspeed.com